A CHRISTIAN PERSPECTIVE ON

EUTHANASIA

RAYMOND L. HARTWIG

CPH.
SAINT LOUIS

Edited by Rodney L. Rathmann
Cover photo (i.v.) by M. Heron / The Stock Market

Write to the Library for the Blind, 1333 S. Kirkwood Rd. St. Louis, MO
63122-7295 to obtain this study in braille or large print for the visually
impaired. Allow 12–16 weeks for processing.

CONTENTS

PREFACE

ABOUT THE CHRISTIAN PERSPECTIVE SERIES

How often haven't each of us been confronted with an issue that challenges us? It nags at our patience, frustrating us in our desire to honor God in the way we handle, manage, and react to the issue in our daily lives. We struggle unable to find the right approach or perspective. Some issues may even cause us to question God and His power and presence in our lives. At times we may feel helpless and weak in the way we react to an issue—baby Christians wondering if we will ever grow up. Feeling unworthy and ill-equipped to be the witnesses of Jesus in an unreceptive or apathetic world, we may echo the sentiments of Agur of old who marveled at the greatness of God in comparison with his own inadequacies. He said,

> "I am the most ignorant of men; I do not have a man's understanding. I have not learned wisdom, nor have I knowledge of the Holy One. Who has gone up to heaven and come down? Who has gathered up the wind in the hollow of His hands? Who has wrapped up the waters in His cloak? Who has established all the ends of the earth? What is His name, and the name of His son? Tell me if you know!" (Proverbs 30:2–4).

Fortunately, God didn't leave us alone to struggle with those things that challenge us and cause us to pause when we don't know what to think or how to respond. With a love for us that reaches back before the beginning of time and connects us with a crude wooden cross that stood in Palestine some 2,000 years ago, God cares about our everyday concerns. He has given us the direction, counsel, and power of His holy Word to help us live lives in joyful response to all that He has done for us through Jesus, His Son and our Savior.

Each title in the Christian Perspective series has been designed to provide the insights and reflections of an author who has personally confronted an issue that touches us and challenges our lives of faith in one way or another. He or she has sought the counsel and application of God's holy Word to this topic and has put his or her thoughts and conclusions in writing to give others confronted with the same issue a "jump start" in their thinking.

The Christian Perspective series has been designed in the book-study format, organized in chapters and suitable for either individual use or group study. Following the reading of each chapter, questions have been provided to further stimulate your thinking and to serve as discussion starters if the book-study is being used in a small group setting. May God bless you as you explore the topic of this course.

SUGGESTIONS FOR USING THIS COURSE IN A GROUP SETTING

Select a leader for the course or a leader for the day. It will be the leader's responsibility to keep the discussion moving and to help involve everyone.

Emphasize sharing. Your class will work best if the

participants feel comfortable with one another and if all feel that their contributions to the class discussion are important and useful. Take the necessary time at the beginning of the course to get to know one another. You might share names, occupations, hobbies, etc. Share what you expect to gain from this course. Take some time at the beginning of each class session to allow participants to share experiences and news items from the week that relate to your study. Be open and accepting. Don't force anyone to speak. The course will be most helpful if participants willingly share deep feelings, problems, doubts, fears, and joys. That will require building an atmosphere of openness, trust, and caring about one another. Take time to build relationships among participants. That time will not be wasted!

Find ways to keep the session informal. Meet in casual surroundings. Arrange seating so participants can face one another. Ask volunteers to provide refreshments.

Depend on the Holy Spirit. Expect His presence. He will guide you and cause you to grow through the study of His holy Word. He has promised that His Word will not return empty (Isaiah 55:11). But do not expect the Spirit to do your work for you!

Start early! Prepare well! As time permits, do additional reading about the topic.

Begin and end on time. Punctuality is a courtesy to everyone and can be a factor that will encourage discussion.

Keep the class moving. The leader should move the class along from section to section in the study guide. Limit your discussion to questions of interest to the participants. Be selective. You don't need to cover every question and every Bible verse.

Work to build up one another through your fellowship and study. You have your needs; other group members have theirs. Together you have a lot to gain.

Be sensitive to any participants who may have needs related to the specific topics discussed in this course.

Be a "gatekeeper." That means you may need to shut the gate of conversation on one person while you open it for someone else. Endeavor to involve everyone, especially those who hesitate to speak.

Expect and rejoice in God's presence and blessing as He builds your faith and enriches your life.

INTRODUCTION

The longer I contemplated this writing opportunity, the more I hesitated to do it. Euthanasia is such a huge subject, about which much has already been written by recognized thinkers and authorities. Much more is also certain to be written, especially as the U. S. Supreme Court takes up the subject of physician-assisted suicide and writes what will be the most significant statement on the subject for years to come. Therefore to join the crowd and write some little thing more has felt quite presumptuous.

Each time I hesitated to write, however, I was also not at peace, for I recognized urgency and opportunity in writing on this subject, the urgency to speak up regarding a hugely significant moral issue and the opportunity to make even a small contribution. Giving it more thought, I also recognized a need for someone to speak from experience and from the level of those people who increasingly face the issue of euthanasia in real-life situations.

To speak of euthanasia from personal experience suggests, of course, either wry humor or self-incrimination. I will speak from 17 years and a variety of experiences as a parish pastor, very much my own independent study of euthanasia. As I share a few of those moments from my ministry, perhaps my learning experiences will also contribute to similar education for others.

1

LIFE IN PERSPECTIVE

OF VALUE AND MEANING

Human reason leads us to conclude that human life results from random, evolutionary processes. Therefore, promiscuous sexuality, reproduction, rearing of offspring, and providing care for those unable to care for themselves can be regarded as choices to be rendered according to the benefit offered to the individual or to society as a whole.

In 1904, adventure writer Jack London published his classic novel *The Sea Wolf*. The plot of the novel involves a young man who, upon becoming shipwrecked, is rescued by a seal-hunting ship called the *Ghost*. The captain of the *Ghost*, Wolf Larsen is a cruel though intelligent man who impresses the main character into service as a helper in the kitchen. More than once as the story unfolds, Larsen puts the men of his crew into dangerous situations solely to see how they will respond. After one such episode, the captain engages the main character in the following conversation about the value of human life.

"You were looking squeamish this afternoon," [Wolf] began. "What was the matter?"

I could see that he knew what had made me ... sick ..., that he was trying to draw me, and I answered, "It was because of the brutal treatment of that boy."

He gave a short laugh. "Like seasickness, I suppose. Some men are subject to it, and others are not."

"Not so," I objected.

"Just so," he went on. "The earth is as full of brutality as the sea is full of motion. And some men are made sick by the one, and some by the other. That's the only reason."

"But you, who make a mock of human life, don't you place any value upon it whatever?" I demanded.

"Value? What value?" He looked at me, and though his eyes were steady and motionless, there seemed a cynical smile in them. "What kind of value? How do you measure it? Who values it?"

"I do," I made answer.

"Then what is it worth to you? Another man's life, I mean. Come, now, what is it worth?"

The value of life? How could I put a tangible value upon it? Somehow I, who have always had expression, lacked expression when with Wolf Larsen. I have since determined that a part of it was due to the man's personality but that the greater part was due to his totally different outlook. Unlike other materialists I had met and with whom I had something in common to start on, I had nothing in common with him. Perhaps, also, it was the elemental simplicity of his mind that baffled me. He drove so directly to the core of the matter, divesting a question always of all superfluous details, and with such an air of finality, that I seemed to find myself struggling in deep water with no footing under me. Value of life? How could I answer the question on the spur of the moment? the sacredness of life I had accepted as axiomatic. That it was intrinsically valuable was a truism I had never questioned. But when he challenged the truism I was speechless.

"We were talking about this yesterday," he said. "I held that life was a ferment, a yeasty something which devoured life that it might live, and that living was merely successful piggishness. Why, if there is anything in supply and demand, life is the cheapest thing in the world. There is only so much water, so much earth, so much air; but the life that is demanding to be born is limitless. Nature is a spendthrift. Look at the fish and their millions of eggs. For that matter, look at you and me. In our loins are the possibilities of millions of lives. Could we but find time and opportunity and utilize the last bit and every bit of the unborn life that is in us, we could become the fathers of nations and populate continents. Life? Bah! It has no value. Of cheap things it is the cheapest. Everywhere it goes begging. Nature spills it out with a lavish hand. Where there is room for one life, she sows a thousand lives, and it's life eats life till the strongest and most piggish life is left."

"You have read Darwin," I said. "But you read him misunderstandingly when you conclude that the struggle for existence sanctions your wanton destruction of life."

He shrugged his shoulders. "You know you only mean that in relation to human life, for of the flesh and the fowl and the fish you destroy as much as I or any other man. And human life is in nowise different, though you feel it is and think that you reason why it is. Why should I be parsimonious with this life which is cheap and without value? There are more sailors than there are ships on the sea for them, more workers than there are factories or machines for them. Why, you who live on the land know that you house your poor people in the slums of cities and loose famine and pestilence upon them and that there still remain more poor people, dying for want of a crust of bread and a bit of meat—which is life destroyed—than you know what to do with. Have you ever seen the London dockers fighting like wild beasts for a chance to work?"

He started for the companion stairs but turned his head for a final word. "Do you know that only value life has is what life puts upon itself? And it is of course overestimated, since it is of necessity prejudiced in its own favor. Take that man I had aloft. He held on as if he were a precious thing, a treasure beyond diamonds or rubies. To you? No. To me? Not at all. To himself? Yes. But I do not accept his estimate. He sadly overrates himself. There is plenty more life demanding to be born. Had he fallen and dripped his brains upon the deck like honey from the comb, there would have been no loss to the world. He was worth nothing to the world. The supply is too large. To himself only was he of value, and to show how fictitious even this value was, being dead he is unconscious that he has lost himself. He alone rated himself beyond diamonds and rubies. Diamonds and rubies are gone, spread out on the deck to be washed away by a bucket of seawater, and he does not even know that the diamonds and rubies are gone. He does not lose anything, for with the loss of himself he loses the knowledge of the loss. Don't you see? and what have you to say?"

"That you are at least consistent," was all I could say, and I went on washing the dishes.

Captain Wolf Larsen has much company in his thinking. Some years ago the small city in which I was a pastor had an abortion-providing doctor, whose practice I challenged in a letter to the editor in our local news paper. He called me at home one evening to discuss my letter.

At that time there was still some debate as to when life begins for a child. I made my case for life beginning at conception and that he in his practice was destroying human lives. His response was remarkable. "Reverend, I know that. But it's like the oak tree in my backyard. It drops far more acorns each year than I want or need, and so I rake them up and throw them into the fire." His point was clear.

In sharp contrast to this self-involved and self-indulging philosophy that values human life according to what it can provide or contribute to society, God has revealed to us in His word a contrasting perspective. For those who know Jesus as their personal Lord and Savior, their lives and the lives of those around them are precious gifts—gifts only a masterful, awesome, and loving God could bestow. Jesus values all human lives, individually and collectively. Though He created the entire universe, Jesus allowed Himself to be born into the humblest of situation as a helpless human infant. During the years that culminated with His supreme sacrifice for the sins of the world, He demonstrated His love and care, touching human lives personally and without concern about going against the mainstream of popular opinion about who was or was not a worthy associate. In His ministry Jesus reached out to the poor, the paralyzed, the hungry, the leprous, the abandoned, and the outcasts—and they were never again the same. Finally, His love and grace have touched you and me and, as His Holy Spirit continues His work in our lives, we too are never the same.

Among the changes His Spirit brings to us is the desire and ability to love one another with a love that mirrors the relationship Jesus continually sought with His Father in heaven and with all others. Jesus summarized God's design for all people with the words "Love the Lord your God with all your heart and with all your soul and with all your mind" and "Love your neighbor as yourself" (Matthew 22:37, 39).

Because Jesus lived, died, and rose again we qualify to receive the benefits God freely offers. Among these is a new perspective about the value of our lives and of all human life. As God's Spirit gives us faith, He also brings us to the knowledge and understanding that all human life has value as God has created and redeemed it through His Son.

1 Peter 2:9–10 records, "But you are a chosen people, a royal priesthood, a holy nation, a people belonging to God, that you may declare the praises of Him who called you out of darkness into His wonderful light. Once you were not a people, but now you are the people of God; once you had not received mercy, but now you have received mercy." The value God places on each of us whom He made His own through faith in Christ Jesus is the same value His Spirit moves us to place on all others as He enlightens us to shine in a world increasingly antagonistic to protecting, nurturing, and treasuring all human life.

FOR DISCUSSION

1. Explain Wolf Larsen's perspective on the value of human life. What evidence of this philosophy do you find in contemporary society? In your opinion, what gives human life its value?

2. Is the failure rightly to value human life a modern phenomenon? (See Genesis 4:23; Psalm 106:37–38.)

3. After Adam and Eve disobeyed God, sin quickly contaminated people's regard for themselves and others. Review the account of Cain and Abel recorded in Genesis 4:1–8. Describe the events leading up to the first murder.

4. Before Cain killed Abel, God warned (Genesis 4:7), "If you do what is right, will you not be accepted? But if you do not do what is right, sin is crouching at your door; it desires to have you, but you must master it." What temptations do we face to disregard the value of the lives of others?

5. For all human sins, God provided the ultimate cure. Read 2 Corinthians 5:14–18. Tell what being a new person in Christ Jesus means to you as you think about your own life. the lives of others.

2

EUTHANASIA: THE PIVOTAL MOMENT

SETTING THE STAGE

I believe the present-day discussion of euthanasia must begin with a look at the early 1960s. I was a student in a boarding high school at the time, in the early years of preparation for the pastoral ministry. I recall being mostly interested in the immediate things of student life: homework assignments and intramural sports and extracurricular activities centered in a four-block radius of campus life. I was only mildly aware of national and world events.

The 1960s have been remembered as stormy times. No one can forget Viet Nam, of course, although as a preministerial student my 4-D classification with the Selective Service left me feeling pretty secure. Like many people, I also clearly remember where I was and what I was doing that moment of the first announcement that John Kennedy had been shot in Dallas.

For many years I, also like many people, would regard the assassination of President Kennedy as a defining moment in a turbulent decade. I can see clearly now that the pivotal moment not only of the decade but for the course of American society had taken place already a year prior to JFK's assassination, with another death, also in Texas. I remember this death too, though only faintly and not with a time and place, for it was unaccompanied by equal national notice. There was no every-network television coverage of mourning woman and children, no black-draped funeral train, no 21 gun burial at Arlington.

The August 4, 1962 *Los Angeles Times* story told how on July 16 of 1962, Sherri Finkbine read a newspaper story about babies born in Europe with serious birth defects after their mothers had taken thalidomide. Fearing that her unborn child would suffer similar defects since she had also taken the drug, "Pretty Sherri Finkbine" set out to have an abortion. Described as the perfect suburban wife and mother, Sherri's dilemma drew the sympathy of many. Planned Parenthood's Alan Guttmacher argued that antiabortion laws "just haven't kept up with the medicine."

Sherri Finkbine went through with her "abortion operation" despite laws then to the contrary. I remember being troubled and confused, feeling dwarfed by the immensity of an action which was openly wrong but which also begged understanding and empathy.

Apparently many people at the time shared my confusion, feeling unprepared to know how to think about or address this major moment in history and unable to recognize its consequences. When a 1962 Gallup Poll asked whether Sherri Finkbine did right or wrong "in having this abortion operation," 52 percent of those responding thought she had done right. 32 percent felt she had done wrong. And 16 percent had no opinion. Most of us that day did not recognize that we had just witnessed the great pivotal event of our time. With regard to life issues in general and euthanasia in particular, the slide down the slippery slope we hear so much about today had just begun.

THE SLIPPERY SLOPE

If you travel into the mountains of earthquake-prone Kazakstan from its capital city of Almaty, you will happen upon a pitiable sight. You will see barricades erected along the way to stop rockslides from coming down the valley and causing even greater destruction in more populated areas below. It doesn't require an engineer's eye to picture those crisscross constructions of concrete and steel crushed like tiny toys under a megaton surge of rock.

Those Kazak barricades offer a concrete and steel picture of the feeble attempts that have been made in our American society to halt the surge of destructive ideas and ensuing moral collapse which was set in motion by that society-shaking event of 1962 in Texas. Patrick Buchanan in his August 1990 article in *The Summit Journal* charted its course down the slope:

> Thirty years ago, Americans argued over whether it was moral for a woman, whose fetus had been deformed by thalidomide, to have an abortion. Now, abortion is a constitutional right: 25 million have been performed; and we argue over the morality of denying food and water to deformed infants. Few may acknowledge it, but we are far along in a process that is altering the character of our nation. The first, critical step was to deny that all life is a gift from God, and that no man can take it; and to assert, instead, our right to decide when a human being is a "person." We did that in Roe v. Wade.

> The second step was to assert that some persons are better off dead, such as comatose victims of accidents whose agonized loved ones want to stop the feeding. The third step is to assert the "right to die," and a concomitant duty, to assist individuals who seek to exercise it. In a Detroit suburb, Dr. Jack Kevorkian climbed into his Volkswagen van with 54-year-old Janet Adkins, and drove off

to a public park. There, he hooked up Mrs. Adkins, who suffered from early Alzheimer's, to his homemade suicide machine. A syringe in her arm, Mrs. Adkins pushed a button that sent two fluids into her body. One left her unconscious, the second stopped her heart. Her last act, said Dr. Kevorkian, was to rise as though to kiss him, and say, "Thank you, thank you, thank you."

And step four: It is reasonable for us to choose it for those who cannot make the decision themselves, i.e., the incurably insane and terminally ill who do not enjoy quality of life. Once all the other frontiers have been crossed, the final one is the great leap forward by the state, when it declares that, just as a mother has the right to terminate the life of her unborn, just as a family has the right to pull the plug on grandparents, so, the state has the right to rid itself of those who threaten the social organism. In our lifetime, Germany, Russia, China and Cambodia have crossed this final frontier of 20th century man.

We not only recognize truth in Buchanan's words. We also recognize that America today is already much farther down the slope than when those words were written, despite all the efforts of well-meaning people in our society to build barricades to stop this deadly, destructive slide. One after another, principles and laws have collapsed under the weight of heretofore outrageous ideas.

Early, critical pro-life barricades hastily erected to save babies' lives have long been overrun by the full force of pro-choice thinking, leaving in its wake wholesale abortion and infanticide, effectively burying under a huge pile of arbitrary justifications the concept of the sanctity and preciousness of every human life. The removal of life support for the comatose has become legal and historical fact, accompanied by ever wider allowances for hastening death for those thought to be dying anyway. Now the murderous rush, already well down the slope, threatens to overwhelm the final barricade, the last critical area of life concern: the rapid movement in our society toward overt legalized euthanasia.

The intent of this study is not to construct that final great barricade which will once and for all halt the murderous slide down the slippery slope. That attempt will be made throughout our society as the issue of physician-assisted suicide is debated and determined. We pray its success for the sake of vulnerable human lives and our society itself. My intent is to point out the real onus behind not only this latest surge but behind the entire rush down the slope. That dark overwhelming force is euthanasia.

FOR DISCUSSION

1. Only some of us will of course be able to recall where we were in July of 1962. If you are 50 or more years old today, do you remember Sherri Finkbine and her dilemma? Do you remember recognizing the moment as significant, perhaps even agonizing over it?

   Would you agree that Mrs. Finkbine's decision to abort her child was the pivotal moment for our society's downward slide which has all but buried the principle of the sanctity of human life? What consideration, today the primary rationale behind many abortions, would you say was the crux of her decision?

2. As Christians we recognize that the most pivotal moments of all history are recorded in the Holy Scriptures. Read again Genesis 1–3 (especially Genesis 1:27–31 and Genesis 3:1–19) and John 1–3 (especially John 3:14–21). Consider again how these words of Scripture put everything else in perspective, especially concerns regarding the value and quality of life.

3. Apply James 1:14–15 to the concept of the slippery slope.

4. Read also Romans 1:18–32. To what does St. Paul attribute the kind of slide which we see underway in our society today?

5. Read Titus 2:13 and 14. Apply these verses to all of us as we reflect on our failure to value God's gift of human life.

3

EUTHANASIA
"GOOD DEATH"?

IN PERSPECTIVE

"Euthanasia" (from two Greek words meaning "good death") is not a new subject. It has a long history and has always presented something of a dilemma to well-meaning, loving people who have watched in horror while loved ones have suffered. Thoughts of euthanasia have a way of crowding their way into caring minds at all such times, offering the prospect of sparing further suffering by an earlier, easier "good death."

Christian theologians, of course, have always cringed at the thought of any death being considered good. Death is, after all, the last enemy, overcome once and for all and at great cost by the sacrificial death and powerful resurrection of Jesus Christ, and still to be overcome in every unsaved human life through Baptism and faith. As a parish pastor well-equipped with a seminary training, I have of course always cringed right along with the theologians at the thought of euthanasia, for all the important theological reasons.

I recognize today, however, that I have learned the most striking lessons about life and suffering and also "good death" after leaving the seminary from the people I served as pastor. During those 17 years, hospital rooms became classrooms, special moments in ministry became powerful next lessons, and real-life situations became the laboratories in which the most compelling truths regarding life and suffering and what finally is the "good death" were demonstrated and underscored time and again.

B

I think his name started with a B. While I'm not certain about his name anymore, I will always remember his story and the lessons I learned as he faced death. My education from B began one winter afternoon with a telephone call to go quickly to our local hospital 40 miles away. There had been an awful accident.

B was a small businessman whose company moved farm buildings. On this particular day he and his crew had been moving a large barn down a highway. The power company was waiting at an intersection to shut off the power to some high voltage lines. According to plan, B, riding on the roof, was to pick up the lines and walk them the length of the roof as the building made its way through the intersection under him. Tragically, signals became confused and B grabbed the lines before the power was shut off. Thousands of volts burned their way through his hands and body and out his feet. Miraculously, he was resuscitated when the high voltage catapulted his body off the building and he landed feet first on the pavement of the highway 30 feet below.

B was conscious when I arrived at the hospital. He was charred from the inside out. It was unknown what organs had been burned and destroyed by the powerful current that had drilled his body. In addition he had more than 40 broken bones in his feet, legs, and back. The pain was excruciating. He begged to die. At such times thoughts of the release of death do cross one's mind.

It would not have been a "good death." In the weeks that followed as I regularly visited and ministered to B, I watched another miracle in the making. Fortified by a very good attitude and a renewed faith in God, B became encouraged as the early prognosis of six months hospitalization and permanent debilitation was drastically shortened and revised. B walked out of the hospital two months later, ready again for a "good life."

As B's pastor I recognized how as the result of the experiences of these two months B's life would be forever changed. I witnessed a very casual member of our congregation have ample occasion to think seriously about matters of life and death and the victory to be found only in Christ and an active Christian faith. It is sobering to think of all that would have been lost had B's early wish been honored. It would not have been a "good death."

D

D, on the other hand, never wished for death, even though he was one of 8,000 children born the year of this birth with the serious birth defect, spina bifida manifesta. Several vertebrae of his spine did not develop completely as his body was being formed before birth, leaving his spinal cord exposed and undeveloped along with the nerves connecting it to the lower part of his body. D was left paralyzed for life from the waist down.

D was already a teenager when I became his pastor. Even before I knew of his birth defect, I of course noticed the wheelchair and the hardships caused by his inabilities to run and play, to climb steps, to get in and out of cars, to just fit in. Everyone around him, especially in the church, was kind and understanding. At times he would even be included in a quickly organized game of touch football in the church parking lot. I very much appreciated the behavior of his friends who were very accepting and considerate. Even more, I admired him and his family.

One day his parents informed me that they were leaving for Denver and would be gone for some time. D was scheduled for another major surgery—the 13th of his young life. They explained that surgical adjustments were required regularly as D's body grew. And no, this surgery wouldn't be his last.

I traveled to Denver that week to visit D before his operation. I did so as his pastor, but I also had a question in mind. After reading and praying with D, I carefully asked my question: "D, is it worth it? Don't you get tired of the surgeries and everything else you face in your life?" Implied, of course, was the question whether "good death" had ever entered his mind. It was a particularly pressing question in my mind, for already at that time the prospect of unborn children being aborted because of D's condition loomed large in our society.

D's answer was quick and unequivocal and offered with a winning smile: "Yes, I am happy and thankful to be alive," an answer also echoed by his parents and family without hesitation. Today, D is a young businessman, partner with his father. He plays a mean trumpet and lends a positive attitude to everything he does. He and his family have never entertained thoughts of a "good death." They only think of his "good life."

D serves as spokesman for any number of people who rejoice in and make the most of the lives they have, even though some judge their quality of life to be lacking. It is sobering to think what would have been lost to D and to the people around him, including his pastor, had his mother made the decision many are making today.

M AND B

From M and B I relearned a different lesson, the very important lesson that life and death remain in our Lord's hands, an essential truth in any consideration of euthanasia. Both were elderly women when I served them as their pastor. Both were hospitalized at nearly the same time. I officiated for both of their funerals.

M lived a quiet life alone in her home in our small rural community. Hers was a neat little "grandma's house," the kind with a place for everything and everything in its place. She was in good health and active in church and community. I was called to the hospital the day she fell in her home.

Her hip was broken, to me a seemingly routine kind of situation. When I arrived in her room, she spoke of never returning home. She was certain that she was dying. I tried to reassure her that her injury was almost routine, that doctors know how to repair these broken bones, that certainly her body would heal, and that many people with broken hips return home to live as before. As I read to her and prayed with her, I was confident that people don't die from broken hips.

But I was wrong. Although M's hip was repaired, her condition did not improve. I remember the day I went to visit her in the hospital and found her bed empty. I remember even thinking that she must have already gone home or to a nursing home. I was surprised to learn that she had gone to her heavenly home. I learned an important lesson from M about life and death being in our Lord's hands.

That lesson was even more pronounced in the case of B. She was also elderly. B was hospitalized for internal medical reasons followed by complications. As I visited her regularly, I could see the downward progression of her condition.

When I received the telephone call one afternoon to go to the hospital quickly, I found B no longer awake and her family gathered around her bed. They had been told that Grandma's systems had largely shut down, that her kidneys were no longer functioning, that there was nothing more to be done medically, that the doctors had decided to remove all of her medications to allow her to die in peace. We prayed for God's intervention but, should it be His will, also for her safe and secure passage to her heavenly home.

I returned home that afternoon, expecting at any time the telephone call to meet with the family and make the arrangements for B's funeral. When morning came and there was still no call, I returned to the hospital and found B fully awake, sitting up in bed, and—to the amazement of all—eating breakfast. She recuperated within days and returned home to resume her life with her family and friends. Some called it a miracle. Others gave blame to the doctors for improperly medicating. I learned an important lesson from B about life and death being clearly in our Lord's hands.

A

I learned the most important lesson about "good death," however, from A. I had ample opportunity to learn, for I spent more time in her hospital rooms than with any other member of the seven congregations I served during my years of parish ministry.

A was a young middle-aged woman of our congregation. She and her husband lived a comfortable life complete with successful children and several new grandchildren. She was just beginning to struggle with serious illness when I became her pastor.

A had been diagnosed as suffering from lupus. There was also talk of rheumatoid arthritis. Her treatment over the next years became increasingly intensive, including doses, more doses, and ultimately megadoses of every available drug thought to give her some relief. Each carried its own price in terms of side effects and misery.

In the years of illness that followed, A and her family lived the proverbial roller-coaster life, A's difficult days slowly winning out over her good days. Eventually, she was only able to make it home for a day at a time and after a while only for holidays. She spent most of the rest of her time being shuttled between care facilities, a tiring and seemingly endless ritual that went on for weeks, months, and then years.

A was an amazing Christian person. Throughout her illness she was always pleasant to her husband and family, to the people who cared for her, and also to her pastor to whom she regularly expressed her gratefulness for his visits and ministry. Although her pain was always considerable and at times even extreme, never was heard a discouraging word. Instead there was the constant though sometimes difficult smile.

At long last the day came when it was clear that she was in her final hospital room. As her heart became weaker and weaker, I was privileged to spend those last hours with her and her family while she moved in and out of consciousness. Moments awake were filled with quiet conversations, with loving words and tender care from her husband, and with familiar words of Scripture and prayer. Then the angels came and carried her soul safely home.

One of the great privileges of the pastoral ministry is the privilege of being present at such times, those life and death times, those most significant moment of life times, to realize the presence of angels, to breathe a sigh of relief along with the last breath, and to deeply understand again that there is such a thing as a "good death"—a death like that of A, not like that of euthanasia.

FOR DISCUSSION

1. Psalm 90 is good reading for serious Christians when addressing life and death matters. The psalmist makes it clear who is responsible for human life. It is finally the Lord who gives and who takes away, however that works out in people's lives. Which verse(s) from Psalm 90 have special significance as you reflect upon God's gift of life to you?

2. The witness of many of God's faithful people who live with the challenges of advanced age, teaches that the waning years of life can be important. One of many serious concerns raised against euthanasia is its purposeful shortening of life and therefore of opportunity for important things to happen. Hastened death robs loved ones and communities of opportunities to care and to learn. Hastened death also robs victims of the most significant moments of life when the reality of death cannot be ignored and concerns of temporal and especially eternal significance command attention. Comment on the Christian witness of persons of your knowledge or acquaintance who are advanced in years.

3. Read Isaiah 38. How did Hezekiah respond as the result of his "near death" experience?

4. Read John 9:1–3. How was the work of God displayed in the life of the man born blind? How has the work of God been displayed in your life?

5. As medical know-how and technology become increasingly sophisticated and capable of prolonging life, what parallel concern should also be taken into consideration with end of life decision making? As decisions are made regarding treatment and care, how important is the knowledge that God in Christ forgives us when we fail to always make the best decisions?

4

"GOOD DEATH" FOR WHOM?

Interest in euthanasia in times past has been primarily altruistic, a last resort consideration on the part of family and friends looking on while loved ones grievously suffer. At such times, desperate people dealing with desperate situations want to do something, anything, even the extreme, to provide relief when death seemed immanent anyway. While even under such conditions the notion of a "good death" must be challenged, as noted in the previous chapter, we can probably understand such feelings and temptations.

It should be good news, then, to hear that modern medicine has progressed to the point of being able to control if not relieve most pain. As the medical community continues to learn to use the resources increasingly available to it, we might logically anticipate that euthanasia, "good death," will soon become an issue of the past.

Such, however, is not the case. Instead, the great surge down the slippery slope has brought our society and world to the point of debating whether physician-assisted suicide and other forms of overt euthanasia should be legalized and regularly utilized. Rather than relegated to the trash heap of out-of-date notions, the discussion of euthanasia has been revitalized as perhaps never before.

A closer examination reveals, however, that this is euthanasia with a difference. Those current discussions of "good death" beg an additional question: "But 'good' for whom?" While there remain altruists who reject pain management and continue to be interested in relieving pain and suffering through euthanasia, it is also clear that today the "good" that is being furthered by advocating an early death does not always have the victim primarily in mind.

G

G was a wonderful lady, a faithful wife, and a loving mother and grandmother. She was also an efficient housekeeper, a wonderful cook, a productive gardener, a community person, an excellent church member, a caring church organist for many years, a friend of our family, and a spoiler of our children. That was the G we knew while I was her pastor.

G's health began to fail not long after. I heard that she slowly but surely entered the dark valley of Alzheimer's disease with its gradually darkening of her awareness of people and things going on around her. As with all Alzheimer's victims, the expense of caring for her in terms of pride and patience and pocketbook increased for her husband and family along with her illness.

I heard how G's husband faithfully and dutifully cared for her throughout her illness. I heard also that her daughter and her husband moved back close to home upon their retirement to be close and helpful. In due time, God in His mercy took His faithful Christian servant home.

G's story is not unique, of course, and the prevalence of Alzheimer's in our society has given further occasion for renewed discussion of euthanasia, "good death." After all, it is argued, wouldn't everyone be better off if the inevitable were hastened? No doubt similar thoughts crossed the minds of G's family during her illness, especially at particularly difficult times. Such thoughts do cross minds when caring for the sick and elderly. But the question, perhaps most revealing in instances of Alzheimer's disease, begs to be asked: "Good" for whom?

I haven't discussed this with G's family, but I am confident that her family would insist that everyone involved in her illness truly benefitted from the patience and pocketbook required to care for their wife and mother until parted by death. Those can be special times. Even at difficult times, euthanasia would never have been seriously considered by this family. But G's Alzheimer's is good to consider. Alzheimer's is reportedly quite free of physical pain to the person afflicted, the usual altruistic concern when euthanasia has been contemplated. What Alzheimer's is not free from is another consideration behind much discussion today: the burden to family and society. While euthanasia therefore is still advocated in our day, this is not necessarily for the sake of the patient with the illness. The new and more prevalent question today is: "What about what is 'good' for the rest of us?"

The opposite of "altruistic" is "selfish." Selfishness is the primary factor behind much that goes on in American society today and injects itself into considerations of euthanasia as well, whether selfishness on the part of the victim or of the family or even of society in general. Consider physician-assisted suicide, euthanasia's latest and boldest entree into American society.

Sometimes it is the victim who is being selfish, as is certainly the case with many of the early cases of physician-assisted suicide in our society. Depressed people are not always capable of clear reasoning and begin to think only of themselves and their seemingly insurmountable problems. Unable to even recognize in their desperation the willingness of loved ones and friends to support and help them, they need help to look at life otherwise. They don't need license or encouragement to destroy their one earthly life. Premature death for such people, before they have had opportunity to work through their problems, is surely not "good death" for them. It is the epitome of selfishness.

We have the opportunity to observe a society in which assisted suicide and euthanasia have already been legalized. Physician-assisted suicide has been introduced in the Netherlands and heralded as a great advancement. Controls have been put in place, requiring that any request for assistance in taking one's life must be voluntary, well-considered, persistent, due to unacceptable suffering, and include a second professional opinion. Even with such controls, however, the result in the Netherlands has been an avalanche of "good death" quickly grown to huge proportions. In 1990, Dutch doctors reported 2,300 cases of euthanasia at the request of patients. To that number add also 400 cases of assisted suicide and more than 1,000 cases of termination of life without the patient's explicit request. Were all cases reported, numbers would likely be much greater.

A closer look at the Netherlands reveals selfishness run rampant. Behind each voluntary "good death" is found a desperately selfish person, or a subtle selfish pressure from family or physician, or even a subtler selfish pressure from society to be "a good sport" about dying, this in a society where hospice care is no longer a priority. And so a depressed, otherwise healthy middle-age woman loses a second son to cancer and asks her psychiatrist once and then again to be put to death. Her doctor asks a like-minded associate for a second opinion. She is put to death. A "good death?" "Good" for whom?

A man with a chronic disease, whose wife is tired of caring for him and whose family has been watching the parents' savings reduced, is offered the choice of nursing home or euthanasia. He chose "good death." "Good" for whom?

A lethal injection is administered to a newborn baby with a relatively common and repairable intestinal problem. The child also suffers from Down's syndrome. The injection was given to prevent, according to the record, the child's "suffering after surgery." A "good death?" "Good" for whom?

In America we are rapidly losing our collective footing on this same slippery slope. A September survey of 1,100 South Dakota physicians, reported by the October 6, 1996 Sioux Falls *Argus Leader,* indicated that of the 442 who responded, 55 percent said they could not support physician-assisted suicide. But 41 percent said that under certain conditions they could, this among South Dakotans, who—with a smile—like to refer to their lives as being 20 years behind the times.

In May of 1996, the *New England Journal of Medicine* published the results of a survey of sixteen hundred critical-care nurses across the country. Nurses who worked exclusively in intensive care units numbering 852 responded to the survey. A total of 141 said they had received requests from patients or families for euthanasia or assisted suicide; 129 reported that they had engaged in such practices; 35 indicated that they had personally hastened a patient's death by only pretending to provide the life-sustaining treatment ordered by a physician. Not reported were the reasons for these actions. In how many cases were family or financial or societal interests the motivating factors? The question remains: "Good death?" "Good" for whom?

This is a slippery slope. Reports indicate that the Netherlands in a very short time has moved from assisted suicide to euthanasia, from euthanasia for people who are terminally ill to euthanasia for the chronically ill, from euthanasia for physical illness to euthanasia for psychological distress, and from voluntary euthanasia to involuntary. Some people in the Netherlands have already begun carrying a "passport for life." They are not interested in a "good death," should they experience a medical emergency.

There have been occasions in my ministry when I was asked to participate in a family discussion regarding the introduction or removal of life support and also the use of extreme measures for resuscitation. These are difficult decisions for families. These are also difficult moments for pastors, helping people decide when to recognize death and when to fight it. Thankfully, we are people of the Gospel who know that when our best efforts fall short, the God of life and death is also the God who gave His Son into death for all sins.

Also, thankfully, I and most pastors in America have not yet had to minister to situations resulting from euthanasia. Apart from the pious platitudes that most preachers can generate for any occasion and sometimes do generate at the time of suicides, how difficult it would be to minister in those situations when for reason of financial or other selfish concerns a family or society has conspired to end a life just because it wasn't considered "good" anymore.

THE B'S

The B's were a family torn and conflict-ridden. The three adult siblings had a long history of competing with one another for their parent's affections and to outdo one another in life's successes and excesses. After the death of their father, the siblings took turns caring for their mother, who finally died after declining health and a lengthy illness. Upon her death the siblings gathered and reflected together on their relationship as it spanned the years. Confessing their feelings of envy and jealousy, they asked each other's forgiveness and pledged a new beginning based on mutual support and cooperation rather than competition. As they lamented the wasted years, it suddenly occurred to them that it was their mother's long illness and the care they provided her that finally brought them together as a family. "God worked a blessing through our mother's long illness that none of us would ever have imagined," one sibling mused.

The word *euthanasia* itself targets the root of the problem: "good death." Today the critical question is "good" for whom? Certainly not good for the victim, neither spiritually nor for a host of other reasons. And when euthanasia's "good" is seen to lie more and more in its benefit to others, then we really begin to recognize the true ugliness and destruction of this downward slide of our society. This is euthanasia with a difference, drawing its strength from the same powerful evil source that is behind so much that is so wrong in our world: selfishness.

FOR DISCUSSION

1. Alzheimer's is a dreaded disease among us, costing great emotional pain and other expense to the loved ones of all of our G's. How additionally tempting the thought that "she won't even know." But what would have been lost had her family opted for a "good death?"

2. G's family was a loyal, stable family. What can we expect should euthanasia become legal and even be promoted in American society? Apply James 5:5–6 and Philippians 2:1–4 to this discussion.

3. If we are honest with ourselves, we must all confess our sins of selfishness. But for these and all other sins, God in His great love and mercy has sent Jesus to live, die, and rise again for us. Reflect on God's great love for us in Christ as you review Psalm 103:8–17.

4. On the night of Jesus' betrayal, He got up from the meal and washed His disciples' feet as an object lesson for believers of all time about how the love of God and the power of the Gospel show themselves in the lives of God's children through faith in Christ Jesus. Give examples of how God's people "wash feet" as they protect and serve all others.

5. The experience of the B siblings sheds light on the age-old question "Why does God allow the sick to linger?" Comment on the B's experience, sharing similar incidents of your knowledge or experience.

5

How about "Euzoasia"?

L

L was a very cheerful young woman in one of my congregations, a good mother to her one daughter, and a major contributor to the success of her marriage. After a number of years another child was on the way, a source of great happiness.

One day L arrived at my office unexpectedly and asked to see me right away. As she entered, I could see that she was visibly upset. She told me that she had just seen her doctor for a routine appointment and that in the course of the examination some pictures had been taken of the child. The doctor had identified some things in the pictures that concerned him and he in turn had informed and alarmed the young mother. The child, he said, appeared to be abnormal, even grossly abnormal. He insinuated that what L carried in her body was more "thing" than baby, and estimated at least a 90 percent likelihood that things were awfully wrong. He suggested that she consider an abortion.

He, of course, was recommending a "good death," good for all kinds of reasons. L, armed and bolstered by prayer and her Christian faith, nevertheless carried the child to full term. Her imagination, of course, went wild, and she pictured in her mind some kind of hairy thing in her womb. She could not look forward to the birth of her second child, very much afraid of what she would have to face in the delivery room.

In due time the child was born, a beautiful little boy with lots of hair in the right place, the right number of fingers and toes, and nothing at all out of order. Prepared for the worst, L received the best, and, with the child, also a sobering thought: What if she had followed the advice of the doctor?

L's case was repeated again and yet again with two other young mothers in my circles of experience, suggesting that her story is repeated quite often in our society. In each case, these mothers gave birth to perfectly healthy babies. That in itself is alarming. At times, however, not all is right with the child. What then? Very revealing are the words of the doctor, speaking of the "good" to be accomplished by destroying a life that is less than what is considered whole and normal. In effect he was suggesting the subtler but very pervasive form of euthanasia behind much loss of life in our society.

I heard only recently from another pastor how a young couple, their child diagnosed as being hydrocephalic, was persuaded by their doctor to agree to an "early birth," before the child would be able to survive. They were successfully persuaded that it would be a "good death." To these cases of doing "what is best for the child" add the remaining one and a half million abortions performed each year, deliberate deaths of even healthy children, pronounced "good" for some reason or somebody? And how many of the partial-birth abortions which continue to be allowed in our society, brutal as they are, are nonetheless pronounced "good"? How many of the cases of infanticide, where abnormal children are left to die of starvation in a remote corner of a hospital nursery, are called "good"? How many of the embryos left over from in vitro fertilization procedures are left to die "for their own good" or used for experimentation to serve some "higher good"?

Many today are concerned over the social ills and hardships faced by many children. Now include a dollar sign in the spelling of euthanasia to include considerations of financial cost to society and note how interest in "good death" increases even more. Hastened deaths of the chronically ill, the handicapped, the elderly, and all who are considered a drain on the economy and a burden to society are more and more readily pronounced "good."

K AND C

When their father lay in a hospital bed the final days of his life, K and C talked quietly together about the careful attention to detail that characterized their father's life. He was thinking of them in this situation 10 years ago when he wrote his living will, they mused. Soon the hospital personnel would disconnect the tubes bringing nutrition and water to his illness-ravaged body and he would leave them. He knew we would have a difficult time making decisions about his care; he knew we wouldn't want to see him linger. And so they consoled themselves.

Ours is, of course, just one slippery slope among many. Like the Netherlands, others of today's societies are already farther down the decline. While teaching at a seminary in St. Petersburg, Russia, I was told that Russian women undergo an average of 13–18 abortions in their lifetimes, in the interest, they were told, of a higher "good." With the Soviet system largely gone, the plight of these mothers and unborn has not improved; abortions provide a lucrative income for otherwise woefully-paid physicians. The notion of "good death" pervades much of our world.

Perhaps what is needed is a new term, one to catch new attention and counter the old ideas. How about "euzoasia," from the Greek words for "good life"? New words get invented all the time. What better reason for a new word than to counter euthanasia and the downward slide of our society.

But if not a new word, then at least a new look. Perhaps the euthanasia issue gives us cause to search God for the timeless truths it contains about the value of human life. From the Bible we learn that human life is not something we achieve or qualify for. Rather, life is God's gift to us and each of us is unique. Human life has measureless value because God loved us enough to send His only-begotten Son to earn our salvation for us by living a perfect life in our place and by dying a substitutionary death for us on Calvary's cross.

Living in America we have the freedom to worship the God who gave all and did everything for us and for our salvation. Yet, as free people we have drifted away from the relationships God would have us enjoy with Him and with one another. A recently published pro-life document, " That They May Have Life," describes the situation as follows:

> American society ... is steadily becoming a society of strangers, obsessed with personal rights and severing the ties of duty, compassion, and love to the weak and unwanted.
>
> American culture has come to favor those who can

stridently assert their autonomy and choice in a struggle for political power. As a result, America has become an inhospitable, even dangerous, place for those too weak to compete effectively in this contest of rights—the young, the elderly, the dying, the handicapped.

American society has adopted a distorted definition of freedom. Freedom focused only on the self and its rights. Freedom from the bonds of community. Freedom from duties of parents to children. Freedom from the obligations of generation to generation. Freedom from the responsibility to sacrifice for others. Freedom even from a sense of empathy.

The ultimate and inevitable outcome of this new freedom is the individual's private, autonomous power to choose life or death, for self or even for others. This is the concept of freedom behind the increasing acceptance of euthanasia and infanticide in American society. This new freedom finds its broadest, most blatant expression in abortion.

Of every three lives conceived in America today, only two are allowed to survive until birth. That which was once defended as a rare and tragic necessity has become an accepted solution to unwanted pregnancy, a popular political stand, and a profitable industry. American law against abortion has not been liberalized or reformed but abolished, with abortions now legal through the ninth month of pregnancy, until birth, under any circumstances. Given this most permissive law of any democratic nation, abortion is the most common surgical procedure in America, following circumcision.

The document then counts the cost of this downward slide in American society, a price beyond mere statistics:

> Abortion has not only led to the shocking loss of 1.3 million lives each year. It has also resulted in a coarsened society, desensitized to death and disloyal to life. America has crossed over the line of a civilized society, approving routine violence against the weak and teaching its children through actions and attitudes that this is a proper way to treat the inconvenient. It can only be guessed and feared how the next generation will eventually treat its aged parents, its handicapped, and its sick.

FOR DISCUSSION

1. Read Isaiah 1:12–20. We notice that the Lord God is very angry, disgusted with the worship of His people because of the blood on their hands. Whose blood is this?

2. Who are the poor and vulnerable, the "widows" and "orphans," of our day? Can any of us who live in America today say that our hands are without stain?

3. In Christ we have a remedy for our sins that are red like scarlet and crimson, for which we thank our gracious God (Isaiah 1:18). In the forgiveness Christ has freely provided for each of us, by faith we are made new (Ephesians 4:20–24). Explain how the newness God's Spirit brings to our lives through God's Word changes us with regard to actions that demonstrate the value we place on all human life.

6

WHAT CAN WE DO?

THE TASK OF THE CHURCH

As God directs and empowers His forgiven people in their various walks and stations of life, He also brings them to desire and pursue the fellowship with other believers through membership in a Christian church. While the first and foremost purpose of the church is to proclaim the good news of Jesus Christ, God would also have His people join together to take a stand when fundamental moral principles are at stake. The most fundamental of those principles is the protection of innocent life.

From God's Word we learn that He has forbidden all taking of human life except in cases of war and capital punishment. All private killing except in self-defense is also rejected. Children are to be actively welcomed and loved. The aged are to be respected, the sick treated with compassion, and the stranger looked upon with concern. These were moral principles in direct contrast with the ancient world where the value of life was often determined by status or strength. They remain in direct contrast and challenge the practice of contemporary culture.

God would have us regard life—even our own—different from all other possessions. As someone concerned about euthanasia has penned, "Life is not a 'thing' to be given or taken. It is a divine gift, to be valued wherever it is found and mourned whenever it is lost."

Because all human life has value, those trusting in Jesus for salvation must speak—both individually and collectively—for all those unable to speak for themselves, including those not yet born, children and adults who may not be physically perfect or wanted by others, and those who may not be able to work or otherwise contribute to society.

Working together with other concerned Christians in response to the Gospel, we can help all who are faced with unplanned pregnancies. Our churches can meet all who are facing crisis regarding past and present life issues not with harsh moralism but rather with a clear Law and Gospel ministry borne out of care and mercy and respect for all lives involved.

The church must also speak for and minister to the elderly and sick and especially to the terminally ill. Many in today's fast-paced and self-satisfying world are considered burdens and obstacles and are made to feel unwanted, unloved, and rejected. Some feel they owe it to their families and heirs to die quickly and without the creation of tension or fuss. But there is no right or duty to take any human life including one's own. God would have His church minister to those nearing death and their families—comforting, supporting, and encouraging them with the knowledge that in Jesus their sins have been forgiven and in the sure and certain hope of the resurrection.

As concerned people of God we must also speak for all who are considered mentally and physically handicapped, recognizing that human dignity and worth are not measured by any socially accepted standards regarding degree of mobility, intelligence, or achievement in life. Abortion of children shown by genetic testing to be "defective" children evidences bigotry in addition to violence. Destroying unborn children for mental or physical handicaps sends the sorry message to every handicapped individual in our society that he or she is worthless and even burdensome.

American history, for the most part, unfolds as the story of expanded protection and inclusion of various groups of people. Yet at least twice in American history entire classes of individuals have been excluded from the basic protections of democracy by laws and courts—Dred Scott and Roe v. Wade decisions. As citizens and workers in society Christians can work to effect a change in our culture's regard for human life. Through our life and witness, first minds and then laws can be changed. Christians have the duty, particularly heavy in a democracy, to hold the state to account.

In addition to advocating pro-life convictions, God's people can also remind Christian health professionals and institutions of their special opportunity to be an example to the world of properly respecting and valuing lives for which Jesus paid the ultimate price.

Christians can also support the cause of life through their efforts to provide women in crisis pregnancies medical, financial, and spiritual support; to adopt unwanted children, including those who are older, handicapped, and otherwise hard to place; to visit the elderly and lonely to assure them that they know they are valued and not resented; to comfort with a loving touch those who are facing death because of AIDS, cancer, or other diseases.

Recently, my daughter called home for parental support. A close friend in her dorm confided in her that she fears she is pregnant. The child's father is unaware. The pregnant girl's mother is advocating abortion as a "good death" rather than have this mess up the life of her daughter. The slide continues.

There is a way to stop a slide down a slippery slope. Never mind barricades. Little constructions are no match for a megaton onslaught. The answer is bigger than that. The answer is to level the terrain.

That sounds like an even bigger task, for even more than a slide down a slippery slope, euthanasia is the evil mountain which gives impetus to the slide. A notion of "good death" is behind all of the assaults on the sanctity of life that threaten to overwhelm us today. Underlying all is a relentless downward thrust of self-ishness.

Leveling mountains like this one, however, is not impossible. The ultimate victory of life over death has already been accomplished, as we regularly confess in our Christian creeds. And this Christian faith is a powerful force which will not be denied a place in this world until Christ comes. Faithfully advanced by God's people it can and will make rough places plain.

Already there are evidences in American society of growing discomfort and even alarm with the slide down the slippery slope. We hear of a trend toward less abortions and the likelihood that physician-assisted suicide will not be readily received. Perhaps the terrain is already changing ever so little. What an ideal time for a strong effort to begin to level this mountain. May ours become a level kind of society where by God's grace each is led to love his or her neighbor as we love ourselves because He first loved us and gave us our lives and eternal life.

For Discussion

1. It happened at a peaceful pro-life rally. An angry man approached a family carrying picket signs and jabbed, "You Christians are so self-righteous! What are you doing to help young women who are pregnant? the severely handicapped? people whose family members lie comatose for weeks or even years?" If you were asked that question, how would you respond? What challenge does the man's question provide?

2. How does Acts 17:25 help us to keep questions of life and death in their proper perspective?

3. At times mistakes will be made in matter of life and death, even in situations approached with the ministry and counsel of a concerned Christian pastor. Apply 1 John 1:7 to a person's suffering as the result of an end-of-life decision they were called upon to make on behalf of a loved one.

4. Explain Proverbs 31:8 in light of the role of a Christian concerned about society's tolerant attitude toward abortion, assisted suicide, and euthanasia.

5. Review the story of the Good Samaritan in Luke 10:30–37. Apply this parable of Jesus to all who by the power of the Holy Spirit seek to serve God in the care and concern they offer to those who are in need of their help.

NOTES